J 636.708
Laughlin,
Guide dogs

Y0-CJG-770

3 4028 08811 3346
HARRIS COUNTY PUBLIC LIBRARY

$27.07
ocn873762553
08/04/2015

WITHDRAWN

Guide Dogs

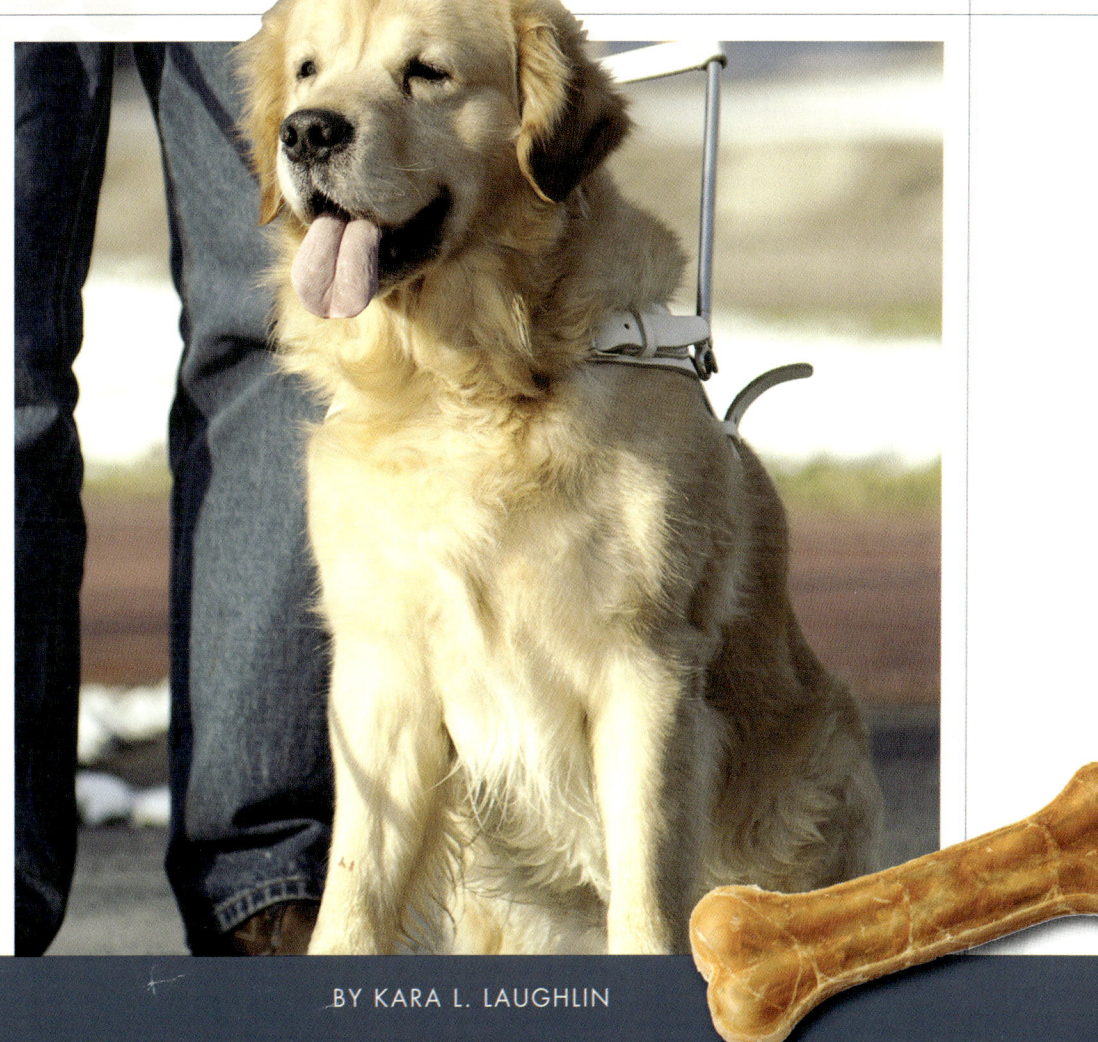

BY KARA L. LAUGHLIN

The Child's World

Published by The Child's World®
1980 Lookout Drive • Mankato, MN 56003-1705
800-599-READ • www.childsworld.com

ACKNOWLEDGMENTS
The Child's World®: Mary Berendes, Publishing Director
The Design Lab: Design
Jody Jensen Shaffer: Editing
Pamela J. Mitsakos: Photo Research

PHOTO CREDITS
© Andrew Burgess: leash; Boris Djuranovic/Shutterstock.com: 21; Chalabala/iStock.com: 8; Elisabeth Hammerschmid/Shutterstock.com: 11; Jeroen van den Broek/Shutterstock.com: cover, 1, 4, 6-7; Mat Hayward/Shutterstock.com:13; Maxim Blinkov/Shutterstock.com: 16; remik44992: bone; pawprincestudios/iStock.com: 14; RichLegg/iStock/com: 19

Copyright © 2015 by The Child's World®
All rights reserved. No part of this book may be reproduced or utilized in any form or by any means without written permission from the publisher.

ISBN 9781626873094
LCCN 2014934333

Printed in the United States of America
Mankato, MN
July, 2014
PA02219

ABOUT THE AUTHOR

Kara L. Laughlin is the author of eleven books for kids. She lives in Virginia with her husband and three children. They don't have a dog...yet!

TABLE OF CONTENTS

It Started with a Buddy 4

Guide Dogs for the Blind 6

Guide Dogs for the Deaf 9

Guide Dogs for Others 10

Learning to Lead 12

Nellie, the Hearing Dog Hero . . . 16

What Makes a Good Guide Dog? . 18

Minding Manners 20

Glossary 22
Learn More 23
Index 24

It Started with a Buddy

We all need help sometimes. Guide dogs are help on four paws. Guide dogs help people whose bodies don't work quite right. Guide dogs give their owners a way out into the world. They are also faithful family pets. For the people who have guide dogs, they are friends who give them their **independence** back.

This man uses a guide dog to help him get around safely.

Dogs have been helping people for a long time. Modern guide dogs came to the United States in 1929. They came because of a man named Morris Frank.

Morris Frank became blind when he was a boy. He did not like to rely on others to get around. He wanted to be independent. Mr. Frank found out about a dog school in Germany. The dogs were learning to help soldiers who were blinded in World War I. Mr. Frank wanted a dog like that!

Mr. Frank went to see Dorothy Eustace. She was a dog trainer in Switzerland. She helped Mr. Frank train a dog named Buddy. Mr. Frank and Mrs. Eustace opened a guide-dog school in the U.S. They wanted to help other blind people use guide dogs.

Mr. Frank and Buddy traveled the country. They went to restaurants. They took train rides. They even went on an airplane! Mr. Frank and Buddy helped to pass laws that let guide dogs go any place people could go. When people saw how well dogs helped the blind, they began to train dogs to help others.

Guide Dogs for the Blind

Blind people need their guide dogs to see things for them. The dog and the owner need to be partners. Guide dogs help people with everyday things like going to work or going out to eat. A guide dog helps by looking out for danger. A guide dog will lead his partner around obstacles. He will stop at a curb or step. Then his partner knows to be careful.

    The dog and owner use a special **harness**. This harness has a long curved handle on it. The blind person holds on to the handle while the dog walks. The blind person can follow the dog by holding the harness.

This dog wears a special harness that a blind person can hold onto.

Just like other dogs, guide dogs love hugs and rubs.

INTERESTING FACT
The first U.S. hearing-dog schools opened in the 1970s. A deaf woman in Minnesota had a dog that had learned to help her. When her dog died, she wanted someone to train a new dog for her. She asked Roy G. Kabat to help. Mr. Kabat had trained animals for TV and movies. He trained a dog for the woman. Then he kept training dogs for other hearing-impaired people. He opened Dogs for the Deaf in 1977.

Guide Dogs for the Deaf

Guide dogs for the deaf let their owners know about sounds around them. Barking doesn't work. They learn other ways to show what noises are being made.

Say a phone rings. The dog will touch its owner. Then the dog takes its owner to the sound. The dog might even learn her owner's name. That way, it can turn toward a person saying it.

These dogs also learn an **emergency position**. They use it for sounds that mean danger, like smoke alarms. Many deaf people say they sleep better with guide dogs. They know their dogs will wake them if they are in danger.

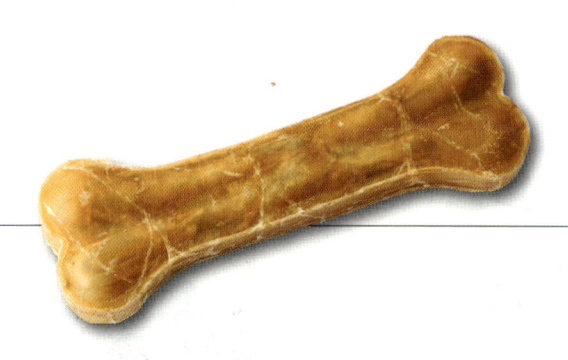

Guide Dogs for Others

Guide dogs also work for people in wheelchairs. These guide dogs open doors. They can get objects that their owners drop. They might even pull the wheelchair.

People with other medical needs use guide dogs, too. Guide dogs can help people with autism, seizure disorders, and mental illnesses.

INTERESTING FACT
Most training programs provide dogs for free to the people who need them.

Guide dogs can get objects that their owners drop.

Learning to Lead

Training a guide dog can take years. Many guide dogs begin training as puppies. A lot of guide dog schools **breed** their own puppies.

Before they begin training, puppies take a test. The tester can tell if a puppy might be a good guide dog. Then families volunteer to raise the puppies. The families take the puppies to many different places.

When they go out, the puppies wear harnesses. They look like vests. The harnesses tell people two things: they show that they are working dogs. They also show that the puppies should go where people go.

When the puppy is an adult, he takes another guide dog test. The dogs that pass the test leave their families. It's time for adult training.

Adult dogs are trained in guide dog skills. Some skills depend on the kind of guide dog. Many skills are the same for all guide dogs.

INTERESTING FACT
Not all guide dogs go through puppy training. Some guide dogs come from shelters. Or a person who needs a guide dog might have a dog already. Then the pet dog trains to be a guide dog.

This puppy is learning to be a guide dog for the blind.

Guide dogs are trained to be alert and attentive.

14

Guide dogs learn a lot of self-control. They learn to stay on the floor of a car while it is moving. They learn to sit in restaurants without begging. They even learn to poop and pee when their owners say. (This is important! When they are working, there might not be a place for the dog to go.)

Even though they are very well trained, guide dogs sometimes have to disobey. What if it's time to cross the street, but a dog sees a car coming? The dog needs to disobey the command to cross the street. This is called **intelligent disobedience**. It is a tricky skill to teach. But it's a very important skill to learn.

INTERESTING FACT
What happens to the other puppies? Puppies who don't pass the guide dog test might stay at the school for breeding. Sometimes they become police dogs. Sometimes their families adopt them.

Nellie, the Hearing Dog Hero

Nellie was a black labrador retriever.

When a service dog starts work, it can help the whole family. That's what happened when Nellie came to live with the Houghtons.

Jake Houghton's mom, Gill, lost her hearing when Jake was ten. Jake had to be his mom's ears. He told her if the phone rang. He woke her if his sister was crying at night. It was a big job for a ten-year-old.

When Jake was twelve, Nellie came to live with the Houghtons. Nellie took over the job of being Gill's ears. Gill was glad. She said, "Having Nellie has meant (Jake) can have his life back, too."

One night Nellie did something that made Gill even happier. The family was staying in an inn. Nellie woke Gill. Gill told Nellie to get to sleep. But Nellie used intelligent disobedience. She got in emergency position. Then Gill knew something was wrong.

Gill sat up. A strange man was in the room! Gill told the man to go, and he left.

Gill didn't know why the man was in her room, but she was glad Nellie was there. Gill said, "I think Nellie deserves a medal for what she has done. She helps me to keep my children safe."

INTERESTING FACT
In 2008, Hearing Dogs for the Deaf named Nellie the Heroic Hearing Dog of the Year.

What Makes a Good Guide Dog?

Guide dogs need to be calm and focused. They need to love working. They also need to be the right size to do the job.

A dog of any breed or mix can be a guide dog. Labrador retrievers, golden retrievers, and German shepherds can be any kind of guide dog. They are big enough to be guides for the blind. Breeds as small as Yorkshire terriers can also work as guide dogs. The trick is to match a dog's skills to a person's needs.

INTERESTING FACT
Today, there are guide dog schools all over the world. They train guide dogs to help people with many different needs.

This chocolate Labrador retriever has been trained to help this boy.

Minding Manners

When guide dogs are at work, they need to focus on work. If people pet them, they could lose focus. That could put their partners in danger.

You should always ask an owner before petting any dog. If you see a guide dog working, ask the owner before you touch the dog. Be ready for the owner to say, "No." The owner knows her dog best. She knows if petting will keep her dog from doing his job.

But don't worry! Guide dogs get plenty of petting. When they are out of their harnesses, guide dogs get treated just like any other family pet. They get lots of love from their families. After all, they are more than pets. They are helping heroes.

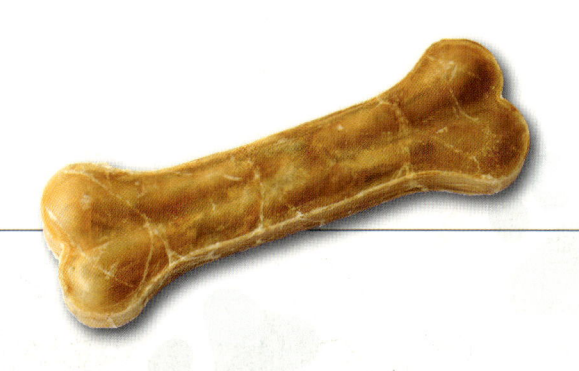

Guide dogs are also pets. They love to get hugs from their partners.

GLOSSARY

breed (BREED) To select and care for animals so that they will have babies with certain traits.

emergency position (ih-MER-jen-see puh-SIH-shun) A way that guide dogs for the deaf stand to show that they hear a sound that means danger.

harness (HAR-ness) The straps, metal, and fabric a guide dog wears when it is working.

independence (in-deh-PEN-denss) Freedom from needing help from others is called independence.

intelligent disobedience (in-TEL-uh-jent dis-oh-BEE-dee-enss) When a dog ignores an order because it would put the dog's partner in danger, it is using intelligent disobedience.

LEARN MORE

IN THE LIBRARY

Finke, Beth. *Hanni and Beth: Safe and Sound.* West Bay Shore, NY: Blue Marlin Publications, 2007.

Laughlin, Kara L. *Seizure-Alert Dogs.* Mankato, MN: The Child's World, 2015.

McGinty, Alice. *Guide Dogs: Seeing for People Who Can't.* New York: PowerKids Press, 1999.

Moore, Eva. *Buddy, The First Seeing Eye Dog.* New York: Scholastic, 1996.

ON THE WEB

Visit our Web site for links about guide dogs:
www.childsworld.com/links

Note to Parents, Teachers, and Librarians: We routinely check our Web links to make sure they're safe, active sites—so encourage your readers to check them out!

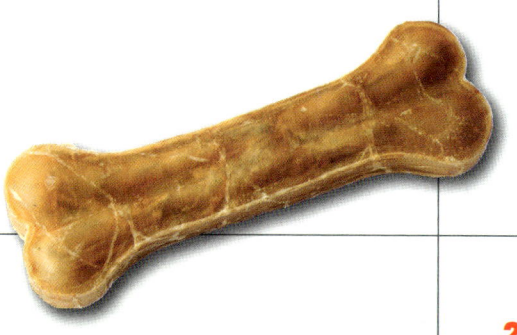

INDEX

breeding, 12
Buddy, 4, 5

Dogs for the Deaf, 8, 17

emergency position, 9, 17
Eustace, Dorothy, 5

Frank, Morris, 5

harness, 6, 12, 20
helping around wheelchairs, 10
helping the blind, 5, 6, 18
helping the deaf, 8, 9, 17
Houghton, Gill, 16, 17
Houghton, Jake, 17

intelligent disobedience, 15, 17

Kabat, Roy G., 8

Nellie, 16, 17

training, 12
types of dogs, 18

World War I, 5

Harris County Public Library
Houston, Texas